CHURCH SIGNS ACROSS AMERICA

ASCENSION LUTHERAN CHURCH LCMS

SUNDAY SCHOOL
9:30 am

SUNDAY WORSHIP
8 & 10:45 am

FREE TRIP TO HEAVEN
DETAILS INSIDE

Pastor: Dennis F. Lucero

STEVE AND PAM PAULSON

THE OVERLOOK PRESS

WOODSTOCK & NEW YORK

CHURCH SIGNS ACROSS AMERICA

PHOTOGRAPHS BY STEVE AND PAM PAULSON

THIS BOOK IS DEDICATED
TO THE MEMBERS OF
THESE CHURCHES WHO
SUPPORT THEIR SIGNS WITH
WORDS OF LOVE

"THE FRUIT OF THE SPIRIT IS LOVE..." GALATIANS 5:22

FIRST PUBLISHED IN PAPERBACK IN THE UNITED STATES IN 2009 BY

THE OVERLOOK PRESS, PETER MAYER PUBLISHERS, INC.
141 WOOSTER STREET
NEW YORK, NY 10012

CATALOGING-IN-PUBLICATION DATA IS AVAILABLE FROM THE LIBRARY OF CONGRESS

MANUFACTURED IN CHINA
ISBN-10 1-59020-216-3 / ISBN-13 978-1-59020-216-6
1 3 5 7 9 8 6 4 2

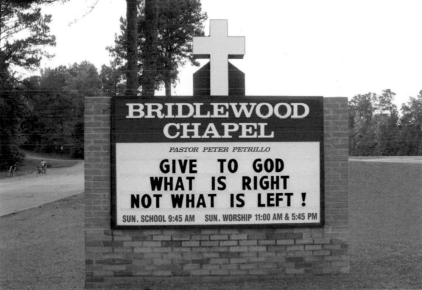

BRIDLEWOOD
CHAPEL

PASTOR PETER PETRILLO

GIVE TO GOD
WHAT IS RIGHT
NOT WHAT IS LEFT !

SUN. SCHOOL 9:45 AM   SUN. WORSHIP 11:00 AM & 5:45 PM

†

OZARK
ALABAMA

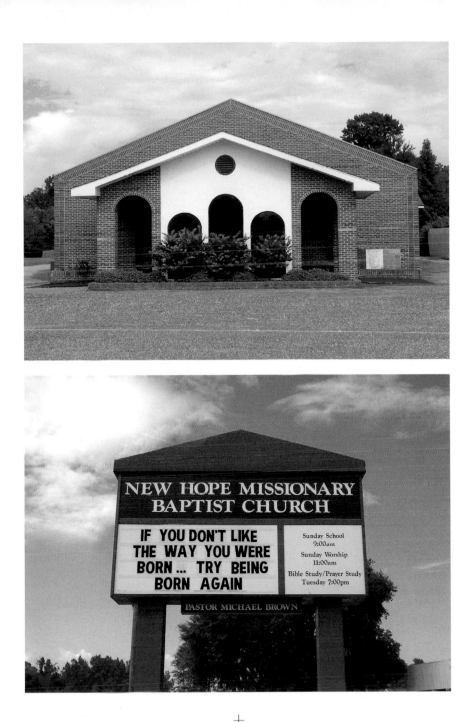

✝

MOBILE
ALABAMA

✝

ROBERTSDALE
ALABAMA

ST. ELMO
ALABAMA

5

CROSSROADS ASSEMBLY OF GOD
JIM SCHULZ PASTOR

NOTHING RUINS THE
TRUTH LIKE
STRECHING IT
SUN WORSHIP 1030 AM

†

ANCHORAGE
ALASKA

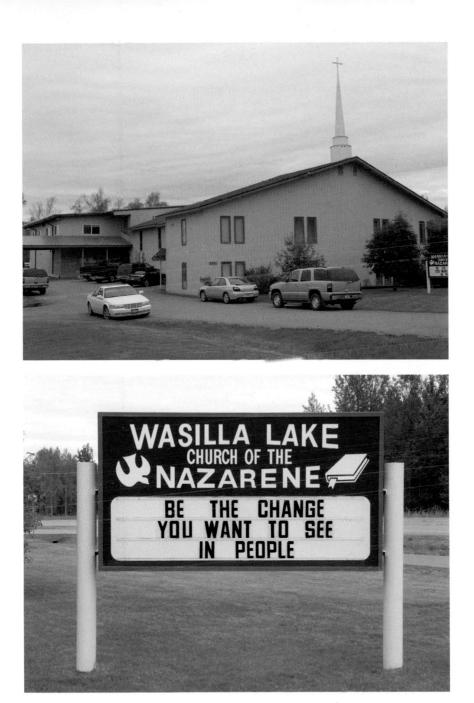

†

WASILLA
ALASKA

PHOENIX
ARIZONA

8

GLENDALE
ARIZONA

✝

MOUNTAINBURG
ARKANSAS

†

NORTH LITTLE ROCK
ARKANSAS

†

LITTLE ROCK
ARKANSAS

EASTSIDE BAPTIST CHURCH B.M.A.

EVERY CHRISTIAN IS
EITHER A MISSIONARY
OR AN IMPOSTOR

CHURCH SERVICES
Sunday School 9:45 Morning Worship 10:45
Evening Worship 6:00
Midweek Prayer Service 7:00

PASTOR Dr. Brad Hoshaw

✝

CONWAY
ARKANSAS

✝

LOS ANGELES
CALIFORNIA

CANOGA PARK
CALIFORNIA

15

†

SIERRA MADRE
CALIFORNIA

16

†

GARDEN GROVE
CALIFORNIA

†

SAN FRANCISCO
CALIFORNIA

Our Savior's
Community

THE ABILITY TO LIE
IS A LIABILITY.
SUNDAY SERVICES AT 8 & 10 AM

†

PALM SPRINGS
CALIFORNIA

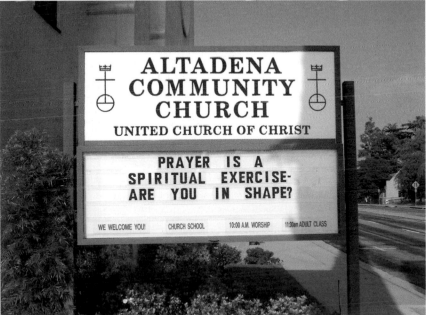

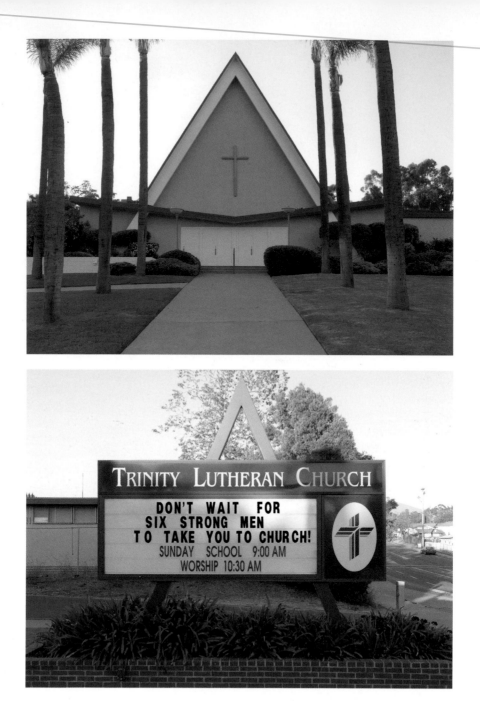

†

SAN DIEGO
CALIFORNIA

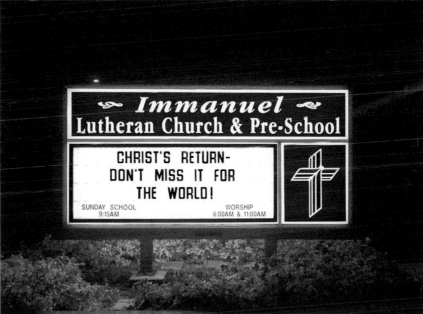

†

REDONDO BEACH
CALIFORNIA

23

First Covenant Church

SUNDAY WORSHIP
10:00 AM
DON'T GIVE UP! MOSES WAS
ONCE A BASKET CASE!

†

ARVADA
COLORADO

25

BURLINGTON
COLORADO

26

WORRY IS THE DARK ROOM
WHERE NEGATIVES DEVELOP

TRADITIONAL 8 AM - CONTEMP. & DEAF 10:30 AM

†

DENVER
COLORADO

WHEAT RIDGE
COLORADO

UNITED
CONGREGATIONAL CHURCH

WORSHIP &
SUNDAY SCHOOL
10:30 AM
THIS WEEK
ALL DRESSED UP
WITH SOMEPLACE TO GO

REV. JIM EATON, PASTOR

EVERYONE
WELCOME!

✝

NORWICH
CONNECTICUT

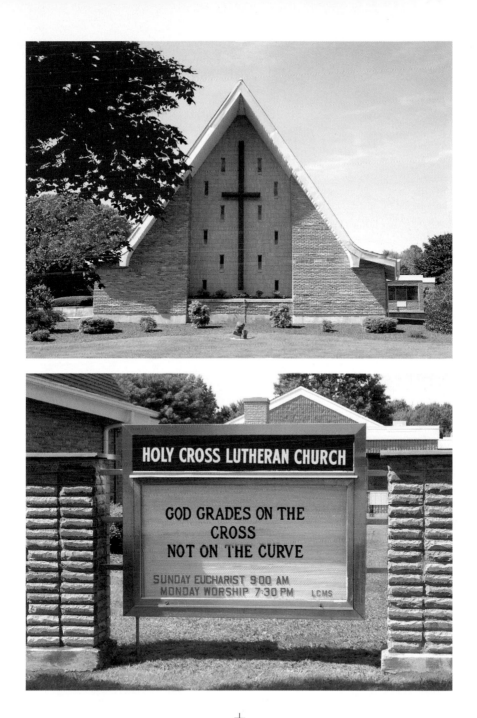

TRUMBULL
CONNECTICUT

TRUMBULL
CONNECTICUT

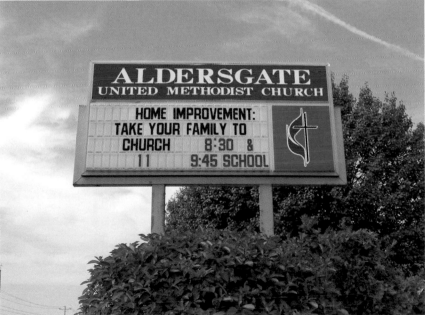

†

WILMINGTON
DELAWARE

33

SMYRNA
DELAWARE

†

DOVER
DELAWARE

CAPE CORAL
FLORIDA

†

FORT OGDEN
FLORIDA

†

FORT MYERS
FLORIDA

†

MOUNT DORA
FLORIDA

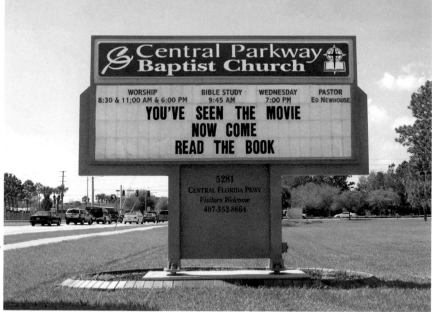

BROWNVILLE
FLORIDA

41

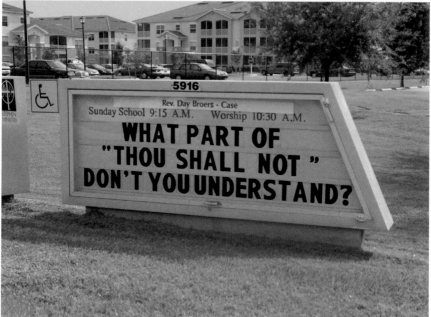

†

FORT MYERS
FLORIDA

42

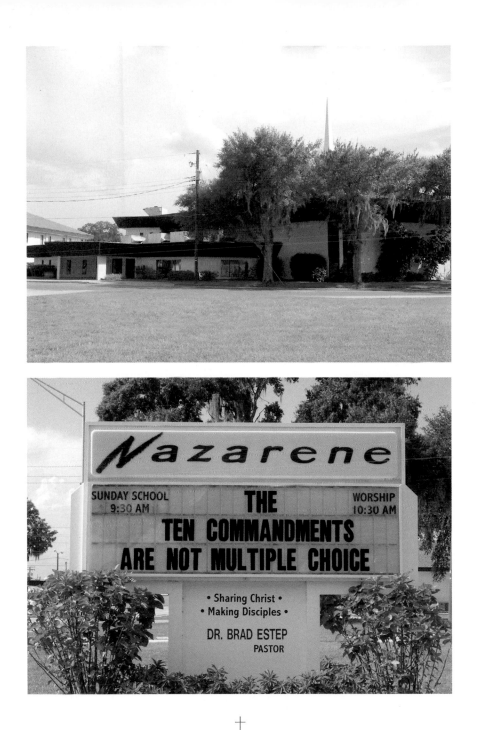

✝

ARCADIA
FLORIDA

† CAPE CORAL
FLORIDA

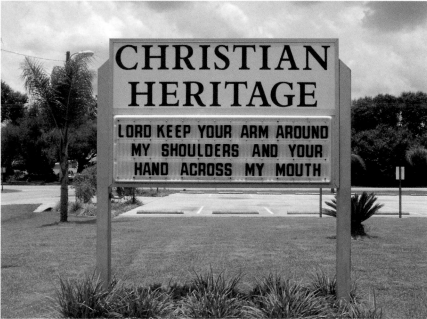

†

ZOLFO SPRINGS
FLORIDA

46

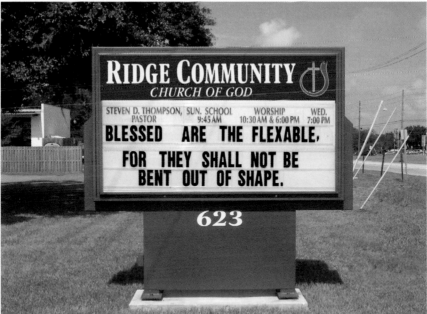

RIDGE COMMUNITY
CHURCH OF GOD

STEVEN D. THOMPSON, SUN. SCHOOL   WORSHIP   WED.
PASTOR   9:45 AM   10:30 AM & 6:00 PM   7:00 PM

BLESSED   ARE THE FLEXABLE,
FOR THEY SHALL NOT BE
BENT OUT OF SHAPE.

623

†

†

NORTH MIAMI
FLORIDA

FORT MYERS
FLORIDA

49

✝

MARATHON
FLORIDA

†

VALDOSTA
GEORGIA

†

THOMASVILLE
GEORGIA

†

VALDOSTA
GEORGIA

†

HONOLULU
HAWAII

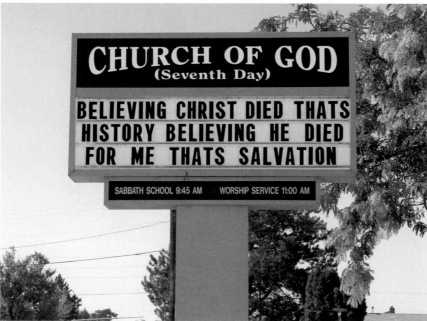

†

NAMPA
IDAHO

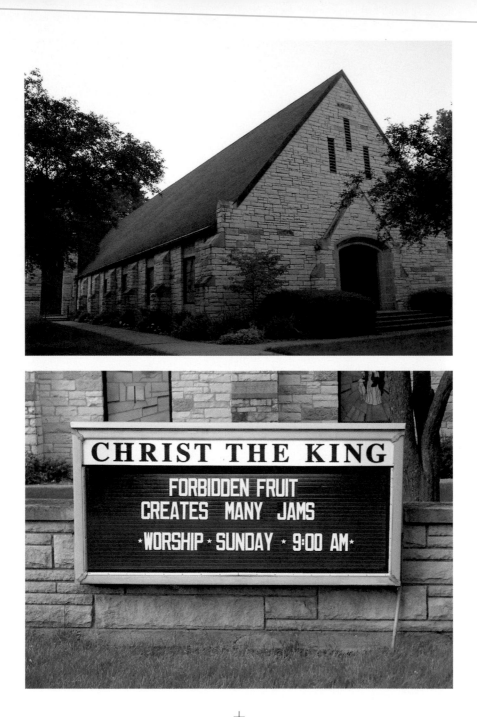

MESSIAH LUTHERAN CHURCH

CH CH
WHATS MISSING
U R
WORSHIP SERVICE 830 10

19901

†

INDIANAPOLIS
INDIANA

60

†

SCOTTSBURG
INDIANA

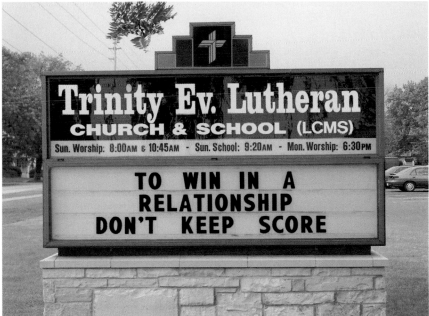

CROWN POINT
INDIANA

FIRST BAPTIST
CHURCH
SINCE CHRIST
DIED FOR US
CAN WE DO LESS
THAN LIVE FOR HIM

†

CRAWFORDSVILLE
INDIANA

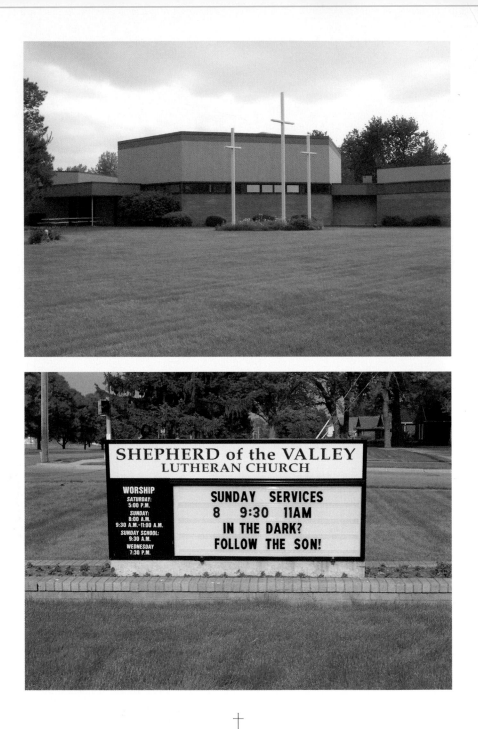

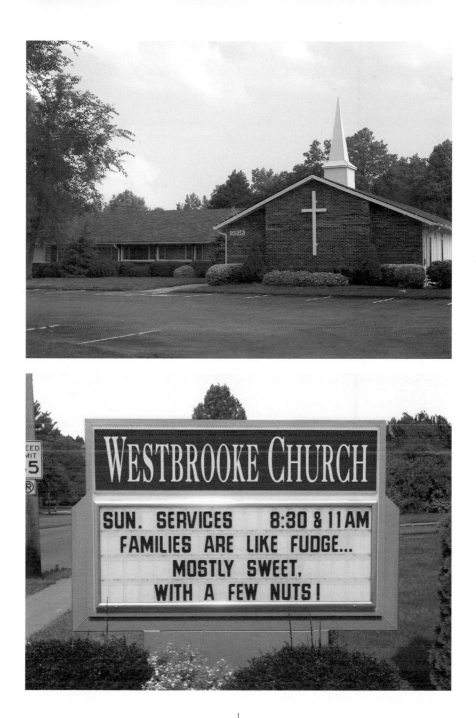

OVERLAND PARK
KANSAS

66

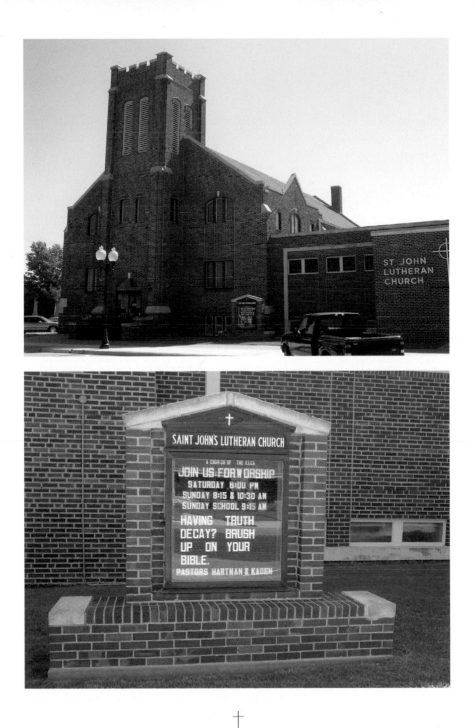

†

RUSSELL
KANSAS

67

RUSSELL
KANSAS

✝

TOPEKA
KANSAS

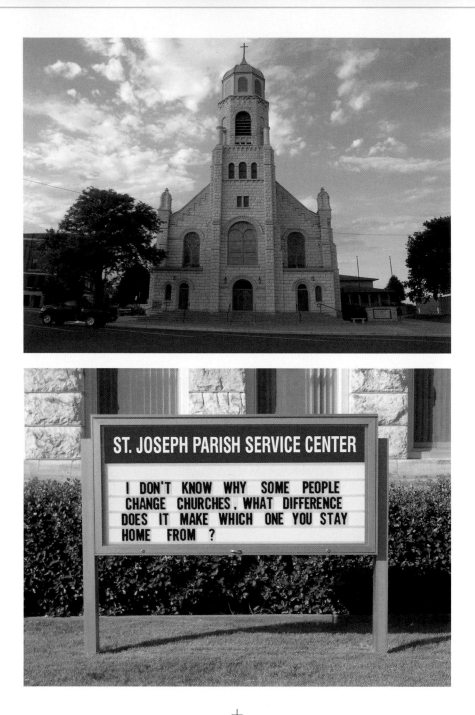

ST. JOSEPH PARISH SERVICE CENTER

I DON'T KNOW WHY SOME PEOPLE CHANGE CHURCHES, WHAT DIFFERENCE DOES IT MAKE WHICH ONE YOU STAY HOME FROM ?

✝

HAYS
KANSAS

70

SHAWNEE
KANSAS

71

†

CORINTH
KENTUCKY

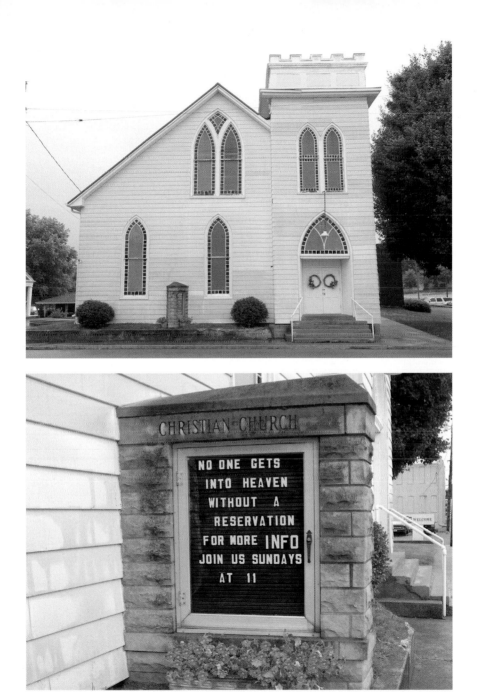

†

HORSE CAVE
KENTUCKY

†

JENNINGS
LOUISIANA

75

†

RUSTON
LOUISIANA

EMMANUEL
BAPTIST
CHURCH

LONG BEFORE E-MAIL
GOD ANSWERED KNEE-
MAIL SEND HIM A
MESSAGE TODAY
COME WORSHIP WITH US

†

MONROE
LOUISIANA

SANFORD
MAINE

†

AUBURN
MAINE

BEL AIR
MARYLAND

†

LAWRENCE
MASSACHUSETTS

†

ATTLEBORO
MASSACHUSETTS

†

JACKSON
MICHIGAN

FAIRMONT
MINNESOTA

†

KANSAS CITY
MISSOURI

92

†

HARRISONVILLE
MISSOURI

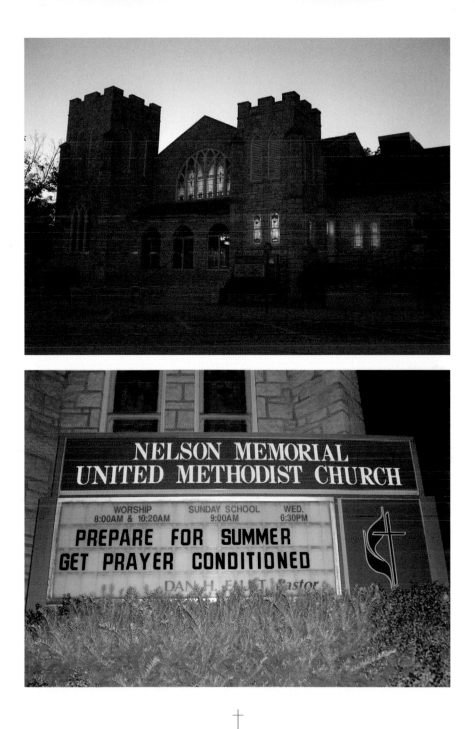

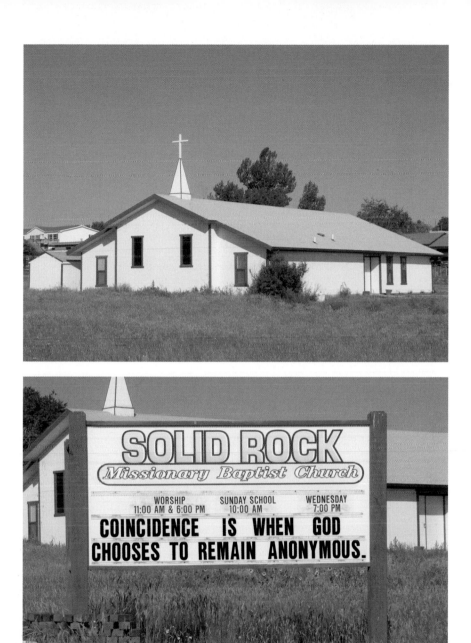

$\dagger$

NORTH PLATTE
NEBRASKA

FIRST BAPTIST CHURCH

FOLLOWING THE PATH OF LEAST
RESISTANCE IS WHAT MAKES RIVERS,
MEN, AND CHURCHES CROOKED!

†

LEXINGTON
NEBRASKA

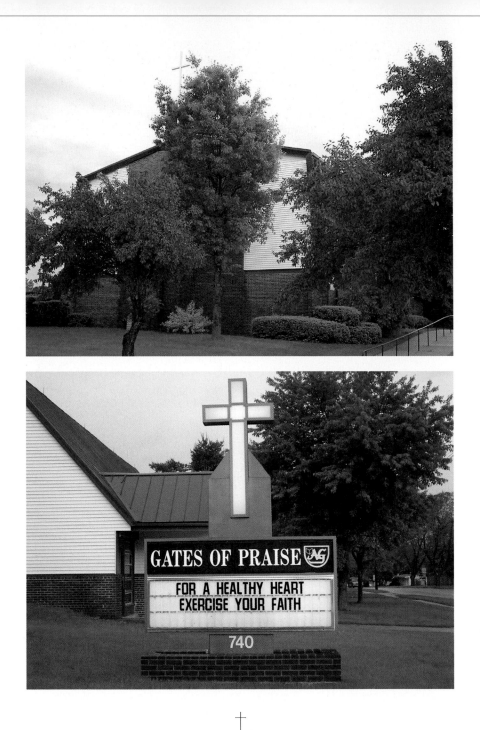

†

LINCOLN
NEBRASKA

100

†

LAS VEGAS
NEVADA

†

SALEM
NEW HAMPSHIRE

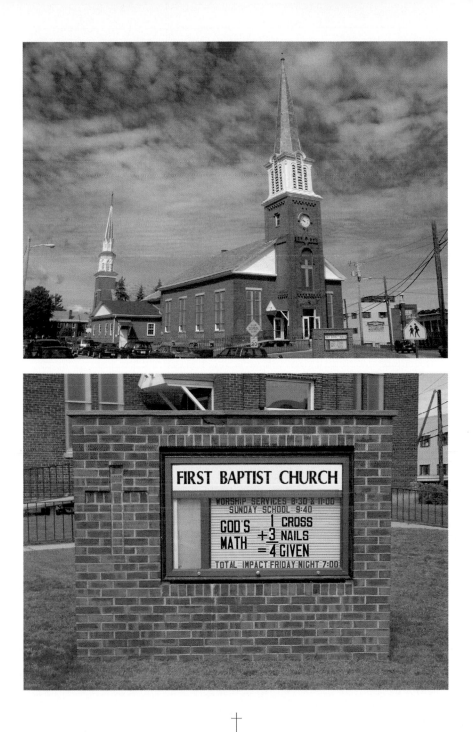

†

CLAREMONT
NEW HAMPSHIRE

PORTSMOUTH
NEW HAMPSHIRE

†

STEWARTSVILLE
NEW JERSEY

†

NORTH ARLINGTON
NEW JERSEY

106

†

CHARLOTTE
NORTH CAROLINA

†

JAMESTOWN
NORTH DAKOTA

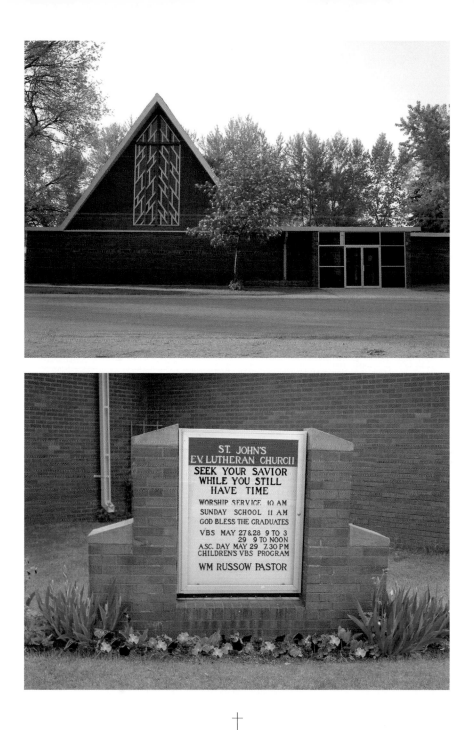

✝

TAPPEN
NORTH DAKOTA

CHURCH OF CHRIST

FIRE PROTECTION,
POLICY
AVAILABLE INSIDE
SEE JESUS!
AT
COLLEGIATE HEIGHTS

Sunday Morning Bible School . 9:00am.
Worship Service ....10:15am.
Evening Service .... 5:00pm.
Tuesday Class .... 6:30pm.
Wednesday Morning Class . 10:00am.
Wednesday Mid-Week Class . 6:30pm

4310

DAYTON
OHIO

†

FAIRFIELD
OHIO

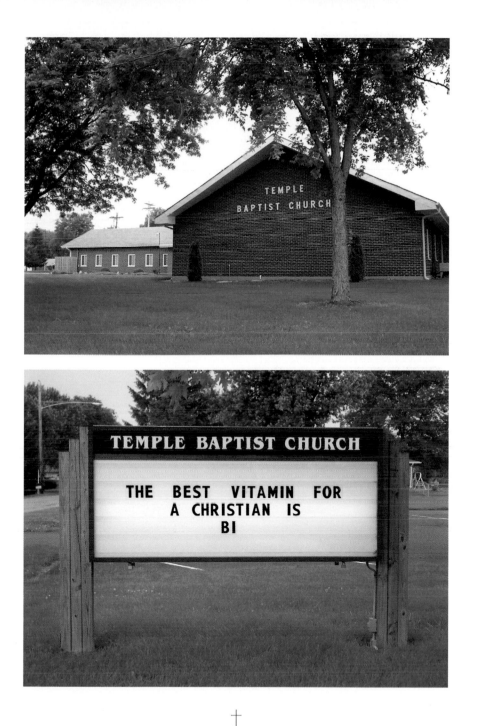

†

FRANKLIN
OHIO

119

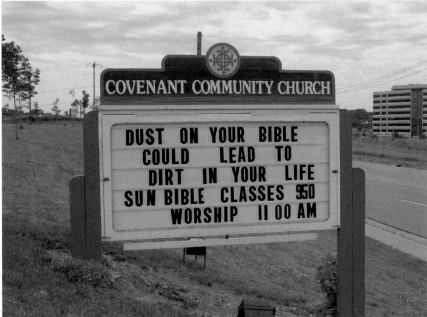

†

GRATIS
OHIO

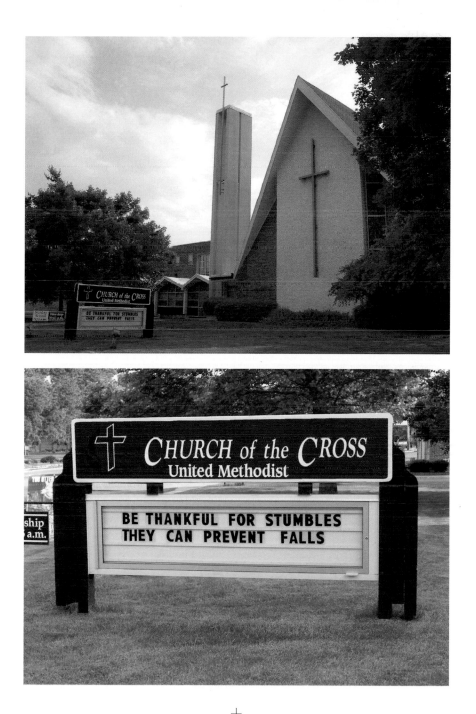

KETTERING
OHIO

†

OKLAHOMA CITY
OKLAHOMA

124

†

LONE GROVE
OKLAHOMA

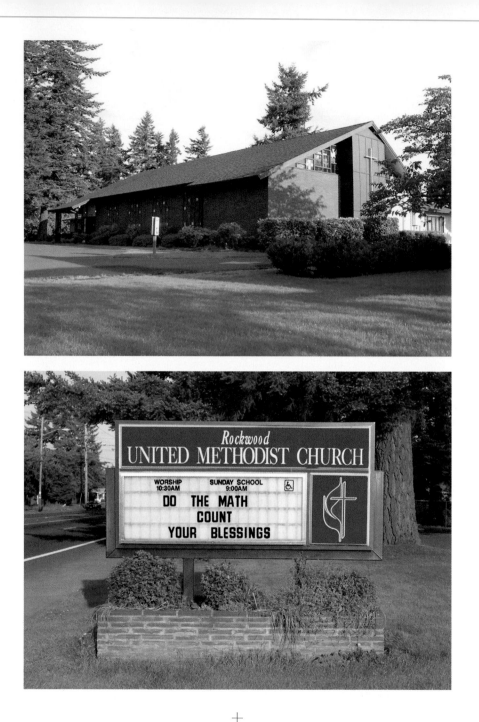

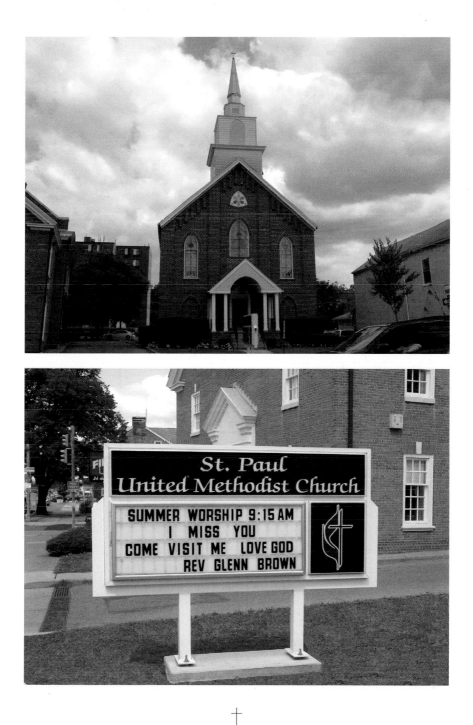

✝

HELLERTOWN
PENNSYLVANIA

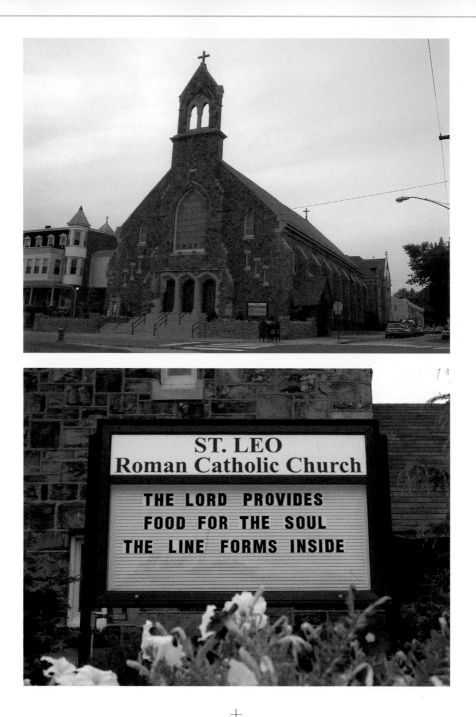

PHILADELPHIA
PENNSYLVANIA

EAST SIDE
LUTHERAN
CHURCH

SUNDAY   WORSHIP
8   930 11 AM 6 PM

MY WAY IS THE HIGHWAY

— GOD

✝

SIOUX FALLS
SOUTH DAKOTA

†

†

ANTIOCH
TENNESSEE

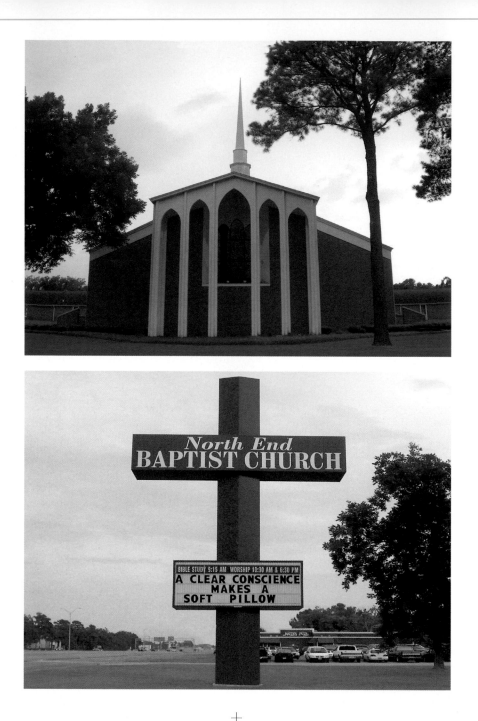

†

VIDOR
TEXAS

BEAUMONT
TEXAS

144

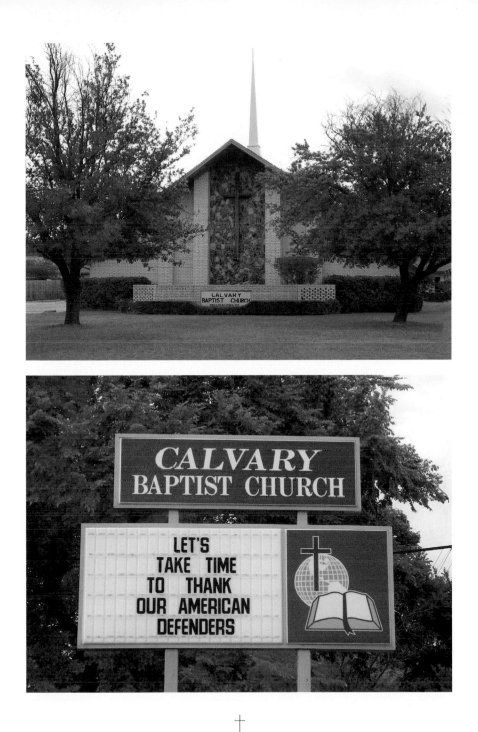

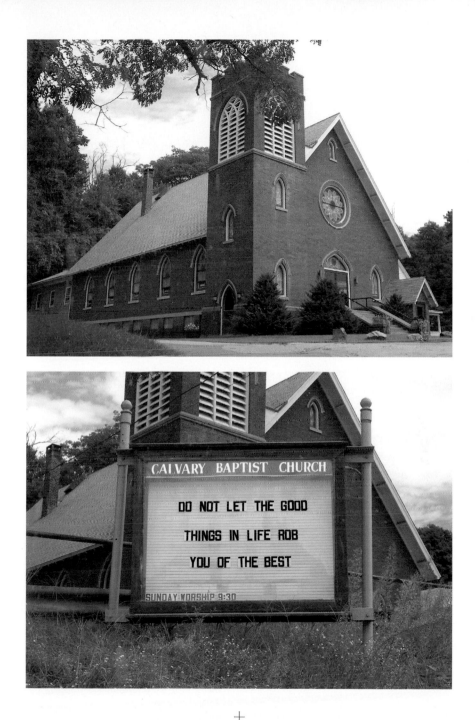

†

SPRINGFIELD
VERMONT

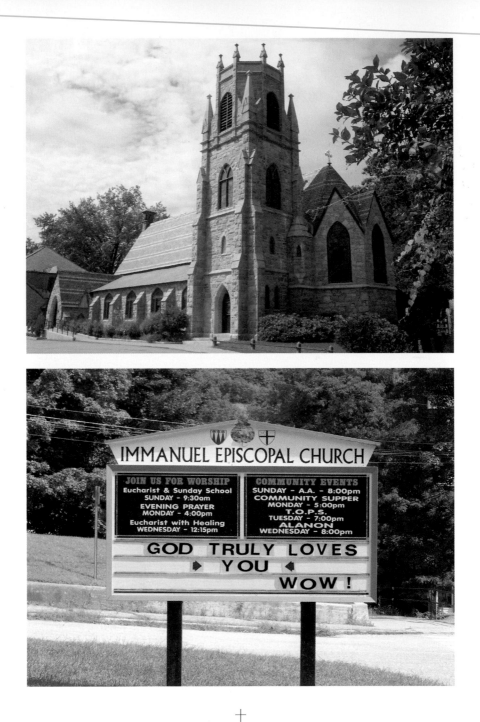

†

BELLOWS FALLS
VERMONT

148

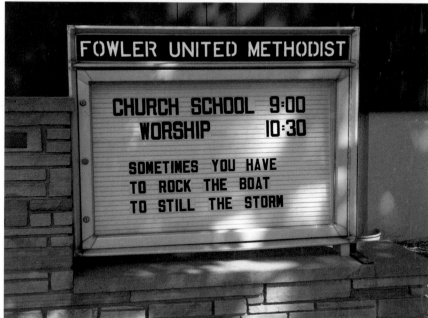

CLEARWATER
BAPTIST CHURCH

SUNDAY SCHOOL	WORSHIP	WEDNESDAY	PASTOR
10:30 AM	11:20 AM & 6:00 PM	7:00 PM	Paul Sandgren

I FEAR GOD.
YET I AM NOT
AFRAID OF HIM.

Design Elements

OL MPIC

†

†

PASCO
WASHINGTON

153

†

KENNEWICK
WASHINGTON

154

†

KENNEWICK
WASHINGTON

155

†

PRINCETON
WEST VIRGINIA

156

†

PRINCETON
WEST VIRGINIA

157

✝

PRINCETON
WEST VIRGINIA

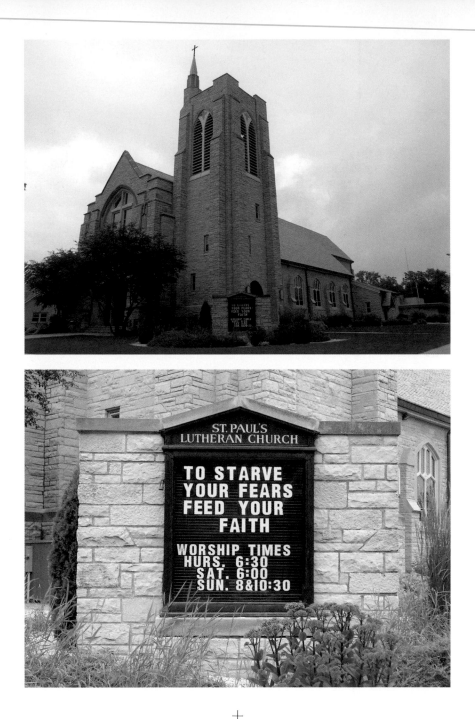

†

JANESVILLE
WISCONSIN

A HEART THAT LOVES
IS ALWAYS YOUNG.

GREEK PROVERB

†

†

CHEYENNE
WYOMING

STEVE AND PAM PAULSON LIVED IN SOUTHERN CALIFORNIA FOR TEN YEARS BEFORE MOVING TO FLORIDA. PAM AND STEVE DROVE CROSS-COUNTRY FOR THREE SUMMERS TAKING THE PHOTOGRAPHS FOR *CHURCH SIGNS ACROSS AMERICA*, THEIR FIRST BOOK.